Winchester Public Library
Winchester, MA 01890
781-721-7171
www.winpublib.org

D1404443

DEER

Amy-Jane Beer

Grolier

an imprint of

⬛SCHOLASTIC

www.scholastic.com/librarypublishing

Published 2008 by Grolier
An imprint of Scholastic Library Publishing
Old Sherman Turnpike, Danbury,
Connecticut 06816

© 2008 Grolier

For The Brown Reference Group plc
Project Editor: Jolyon Goddard
Copy-editors: Lesley Ellis, Lisa Hughes,
    Wendy Horobin
Picture Researcher: Clare Newman
Designers: Jeni Child, Lynne Ross,
    Sarah Williams
Managing Editor: Bridget Giles

Volume ISBN-13: 978-0-7172-6253-3
Volume ISBN-10: 0-7172-6253-7

**Library of Congress
Cataloging-in-Publication Data**

Nature's children. Set 2.
    p. cm.
    Includes bibliographical references and
    index.
    ISBN-13: 978-0-7172-8081-0
    ISBN-10: 0-7172-8081-0
    1. Animals--Encyclopedias, Juvenile. I.
    Grolier (Firm)
    QL49.N383 2007
    590--dc22
                    2007026928

Printed and bound in China

PICTURE CREDITS

Front Cover: **Shutterstock**: Gary Forsyth.

Back Cover: **Nature PL**: David Kjaer;
Shutterstock: Linda Bucklin, Bruce
MacQueen.

Alamy: Daniel Dempster Photography 30;
Corbis: Raymond Gehman 34; Daniel Gulin
14, Eric and David Hosking 18, D. Robert
and Lori Franz 38; **Nature PL**: Louis
Gagnon 29; **NHPA**: Stephen Krasemann 37;
Photos.com: 4, 5, 41, 46; **Shutterstock**:
Tony Campbell 9, Jason Cheever 10, Muriel
Lasure 2–3, 17, Hway Kiong Lim 13, James
M. Phelps Jr. 26–27, Mike Rogal 6, 21, 33, 42,
John J. Sfondilias 22; **Still Pictures**: Ronald
Witlek 45.

Contents

FACT FILE: Deer

Class	Mammalia (mammals)
Order	Even-toed ungulates (Artiodactyla)
Family	Deer (Cervidae)
Genera	16 genera worldwide
Species	More than 40 species, including muntjacs, fallow deer, red deer, roe deer, and moose
World distribution	White-tailed and mule deer live only in North and South America, from Canada to Brazil; other deer live in North and South America, Europe, and Asia
Habitat	Woodlands, forests, and scrub
Distinctive physical characteristics	Long, slim legs; long neck; male deer grow antlers; most have a white rump patch; in white-tailed deer the tail can be white, too
Habits	May be solitary or live in a herd; active mainly around dawn and dusk
Diet	Leaves, grass, shoots, buds, fruit, and fungi

Introduction

There are more than 40 species, or types, of deer in the world. Deer mostly keep themselves hidden away in woodlands and scrub. They have long legs that allow them to run very fast if an enemy, such as a wolf, threatens them. However, with their keen senses of vision and hearing, deer usually become quickly aware of any enemies creeping up on them. The most striking feature of a deer is its **antlers**. The antlers are the bony growths that male deer grow and shed each year.

A male mule deer calls out.

Like all deer, this male white-tailed deer is always on alert.

Deer of America

There are five species of deer in North America. The most common are white-tailed deer and mule deer. These two species are closely related, but there are ways to tell them apart. Mule deer have great big ears just like a mule! They also have a small black tail. White-tailed deer have smaller ears and a long tail with a white underside. When the deer is alarmed, its tail stands up like a white flag.

Elk, moose, and caribou are all types of deer, too—even though they have different names. Each type of deer has a similar barrel-shaped body, with long legs, and two toes on each foot, each with a **hoof**. Most importantly, the males, or **bucks**, of all these species of deer produce antlers. All male deer grow antlers. Female caribou are the only female deer species that also grow antlers.

Extended Family

Deer are related to other types of hoofed mammals. Some of these animals, such as antelope, gazelles, goats, and llamas, look very similar to deer. They have long, slim legs, feet with hooves, and like deer they eat plants. There are two groups of hoofed animals. One, called **Perissodactyla** (PUH-RI-SUH-DAK-TUL-AH), includes horses and rhinoceroses. The other, called **Artiodactyla** (AR-TEE-OH-DAK-TUL-AH), includes cattle, antelope, camels, pigs, hippopotamuses, and deer.

The main difference between deer and other hoofed animals is that only deer have antlers. Some other hoofed animals, such as cattle, rhinoceroses, antelope, and giraffes, have **horns**. But horns and antlers are not the same thing.

Mule deer can be found in western North America and Central America.

A bighorn sheep has two large, curving horns on its head.

Top Heavy

The branches that grow from the top of a deer's head are called antlers. They are made of bone and are attached to the skull. In most species of deer, only the males have antlers. Every year a deer's antlers fall off. It then grows a brand new set.

But antlers are not horns. Horns are what you see growing on the head of male and female bison, sheep, cattle, and rhinoceroses. Horns are made of a substance called keratin, not bone. Human fingernails and hair are also made from keratin. An animal only ever grows one set of horns, which last a lifetime. If a bighorn sheep breaks a horn, it stays broken. But if a male deer breaks an antler, it only has to manage without for a few months. After that it will grow a perfect new set of antlers.

Age and Antlers

Male deer grow their first set of antlers when they are one year old. The first antlers are usually quite small. They are often just little spikes around 5 inches (12 cm) long. Antlers usually get bigger with age, but the size of the antlers has more to do with how healthy the buck is than how old he is. The largest antlers usually grow on bucks that are in their prime, at around four or five years old. A young, strong, well-fed buck will have more energy to spare than a weak, hungry, old buck. Therefore, the young bucks usually have the biggest antlers.

A one-year-old male deer has only small, stumpy antlers.

A white-tailed buck rubs velvet from its antlers on the stalk of a yucca plant.

Shedding Velvet

Antlers start growing in spring. While they are growing, the antlers are covered by a layer of blood vessels and skin. The blood supply is essential because it brings all the nutrients the antler bones need to develop. The skin covering the antlers looks and feels like **velvet**, and that is what it is called. When the antlers have finished growing, the blood supply to the velvet is cut off and the skin dries up and splits. That probably feels a little like when a scab has healed and is ready to come off—really itchy! The deer rub their antlers on the ground or on tree branches to ease the itching. When the deer have rubbed off all the velvet, they have a magnificent pair of bone antlers on show.

Home Sweet Home

Deer live in places where there is plenty of good food. They eat a lot compared with other animals of the same size. They prefer to live in places with rich, fertile soils where many nutritious plants grow. They often live in the meadows along river valleys rather than open plains because the soil next to rivers is usually richer. Rivers and streams also supply the deer with fresh drinking water.

Deer also like sheltered habitats. They have many enemies, so it's important that they always have somewhere to hide from **predators**. You might see deer grazing out in the open, but they are never far from an area of woodland or scrub where they can hide.

A deer keeps
a watchful eye
while it grazes.

17

A Florida Key buck stays close to the undergrowth, where it feels safe.

18

Florida Key Deer

At the southern tip of Florida is a string of islands called the Florida Keys. The white-tailed deer that live in the Florida Keys are very special. These deer only grow to around two-thirds the size of other white-tailed deer. The Florida Key deer are also very tame compared with other deer. They are very used to people and often turn up in backyards and streets.

Fifty years ago, Florida Key deer almost became extinct. Hunting and development of the Keys caused them great problems. By 1955, there were only about 25 animals left. Fortunately, people realized the danger before it was too late and made efforts to protect the deer. There are now around 800 Florida Key deer still living in the wild. They even have their own **preserve**—the National Key Deer Refuge on Big Pine Key.

Line of Sight

Deer's eyes are on the sides of their head. As a result of this positioning of the eyes, deer can see objects and movements in front and to either side of them. They only have to turn their head a little to see right behind them. They are especially good at seeing moving objects, which is why it is nearly impossible to sneak up on a deer.

Deer have much better nighttime vision than humans. But deer's daytime and color vision are not as good as humans'. For example, red and green look the same shade to a deer. However, scientists believe that deer might be able to see the color ultraviolet, which humans cannot see.

Large eyes on either side of its head allow this white-tailed deer to have virtually all-round vision.

Thanks to its huge ears, a male mule deer has excellent hearing.

Sound Catchers

Deer have good eyesight, but they could probably sense someone or something approaching even if they were blindfolded. That's because deer have extremely sharp hearing.

A deer's ears are on the top of its head. Unlike humans, deer can turn their ears back and forth. That allows them to focus on tiny sounds coming from different directions. A mule deer's large ears are about three-quarters as long as its head. These great big ears act a little like satellite dishes, collecting sounds and channeling them inside the deer's head.

Enemy Danger

It's a good thing that deer have sharp senses of vision and hearing. They need all the help they can get in order to stay safe from a long list of enemies. Fully grown deer are hunted by predators, such as wolves, coyotes, bears, and cougars. Young deer might also be taken by smaller predators, including wolverines, eagles, and even alligators!

But one of the biggest dangers to deer is cars. Deer don't understand that roads can be dangerous places. Unlike humans, they don't stop to look before they cross. Scientists are trying to think of ways to make the deer stop and think. One idea is to have reflectors along the road that reflect, or shine, the light from car headlights into the woods. Deer prefer darkness, so this plan might stop them from crossing the road when a car or truck is speeding along.

Born to Run

Deer are amazing runners. A deer's large chest contains big lungs, which help it breathe deeply when it has to flee. It takes a lot for a deer to run out of breath. Although a deer's legs are long and slim, they are connected to great big muscles in the shoulders and rear end. Their legs can carry them swiftly and surely over rough ground. A white-tailed deer can sprint at up to 40 miles (64 km) an hour—that's as fast as a racehorse! In addition, deer can jump as high as 8 feet (2.5 m) at that speed. That's higher than the height of even the tallest professional basketball players.

Running across a road, this white-tailed deer stays out of the way of cars and trucks.

Life-saving Coat

In summer, deer have a beautiful red-brown coat. In winter, the coat is much thicker, but it grows a dull gray color to match the bare trunks and branches of trees. The hairs on a deer's winter coat are hollow, like tiny tubes. Each tiny hair tube has air inside it. Together, the air-filled hairs act as a blanket. They help stop body heat from escaping the deer, keeping it warm in cold weather.

These air-filled hairs also help the deer float. Deer are great swimmers, in part because their coat acts like a life preserver, keeping them afloat with little effort. The furry skins of deer killed in winter were once even used by humans to make life vests.

In winter, this white-tailed buck has a thick coat, which helps protect it from the cold.

29

A white-tailed buck lifts its head while it chews the cud.

Keep Chewing

Deer do not have any front top teeth. When they **browse**, or bite leaves from trees or shrubs, and feed on grass, or **graze**, deer grip the plants between the bottom teeth and the gum of the upper jaw. This gum has a tough, horny pad. Deer feed early in the morning and again at dusk. In the space of a few hours they collect up to 15 pounds (7 kg) of food. They chew the food very quickly and then swallow it.

Later in the day, when the deer are hidden away somewhere safe, they have time to relax and properly chew their food. They cough it back up from their stomach, one mouthful at a time, and grind it slowly to a pulp using the teeth at the sides of their mouth. That is called chewing the cud.

Graze and Browse

Deer eat all kinds of leaves, shoots, and fruit.
But just like humans, there are some foods deer
like better than others. A deer's favorite snack is
the soft new leaves that grow in spring and the
tender green shoots of new grass or other plants.
If you were a deer, walking past a plantation of
young trees or a field of freshly sprouted crops
would be like passing a candy store or your
favorite restaurant full of your favorite treats.
Deer just can't resist the temptation, and that
can get them in a lot of trouble with forest
rangers, farmers, and gardeners.

A young white-tailed deer grazes on some fresh green grass shoots.

33

Farmland fences have to be much higher than this one to stop deer from jumping over them and damaging crops.

34

Fenced Out

Forest rangers try all sorts of things to keep deer
out. They wrap plastic coils around young trees.
These coils stop deer and other animals from
nibbling the tender young shoots in spring.
In winter, deer can ruin trees by eating their
bark. Another way to protect crops is to fence
them in, and the deer out. But deer can leap
normal stock fences as easily as you can cross
over a doorstep. Deer fences have to be at least
10 feet (3 m) tall and very strong. They can't
have holes in them either. You'd be amazed at
how small a hole an adult deer can get through.
A fully grown female white-tailed deer can
wriggle through a hole in a wire fence smaller
than 1 foot (30 cm) across if she thinks there
is something tasty to eat on the other side!

Hunted!

Thousands of deer are shot in North America every year. Some people enjoy the sport of shooting, while others hate the idea. But most people agree that in some places, deer need to be controlled. If they were not shot there would soon be too many of them. The deer would be overcrowded and in danger of starving to death.

Native Americans hunted deer for thousands of years. They understood that the animals were an important part of nature. People that now hunt deer should show the same respect and make sure that whenever a deer is shot, it is not wasted. Deer meat is called **venison**. It is very low in fat, which makes it healthier for you than beef or pork. Deerskin can be used to make buckskin leather, and deer antlers are turned into all kinds of tools and ornaments.

Herds of deer, such as these mule deer, are often shot at by hunters.

There's very little to eat during winter, as this young white-tailed deer is finding.

Hard Times

Deer living in northern areas find life tough in winter because plants stop growing and there is not much to eat. What little food exists is often covered in snow. The deer have to dig with their front feet to find food such as moss, grass, lichen, and acorns.

When all the leaves have gone from the trees, the forest is not as safe as it is in summer. At this time of year, there are fewer places to hide from predators. The deer gather together in larger groups than normal, called herds. With many eyes and ears watching out for danger, they are much safer. They all feed in the same area before moving on together. This action is called **yarding**.

Showing Off

Deer **mate** in fall, when the bucks and **does**, or females, are in excellent condition after a summer of eating well. The bucks spend a lot of time strutting up and down, showing off their antlers. They do this to impress the does and to show other bucks how big and strong they are. Male deer carry out a range of activities to impress the females. They bellow and roar loudly, roll in mud, and even urinate on themselves to put off a strong smell.

If the female likes what she sees and smells, she joins the male for a while. The buck and doe stay together for a few days. During this time the buck stops other males from coming near the doe.

Roaring loudly, a male mule
deer lets the females know
he is in the area.

Two bucks lock antlers in a fight over a female.

Heads Down

If two equally matched bucks both like the same female, the only way to decide which one is the strongest is for them to fight each other. That is what their antlers are for. Before fighting, the two males size each other up. They walk side by side, checking out the other buck's height, muscles, and antlers. If both bucks still think they can win, they face each other, lower their heads, and charge. Their antlers clash and lock, and the two bucks push and shove. Each one tries to drive the other backward—it's a bit like a tug of war, but the deer are pushing, not pulling.

The female they are fighting over watches this activity to see which buck wins. While she also keeps an eye out in case any more bucks happen to be passing, she will usually mate with the winner of the fight.

A Brand-new Life

Baby deer are called **fawns**. They are born in spring. Female white-tailed deer and mule deer usually have one or two fawns at a time, but sometimes there are three. Each fawn weighs about 7 pounds (3.2 kg). That is about the same size as some human babies, but unlike any of us, baby deer can get up onto their feet right away.

Fawns have a red-brown coat covered in white spots. The spots act as **camouflage**. In bright sunlight the spots make the fawn difficult to see when it is lying in long grass. Fawns are very good at lying perfectly still, which makes their camouflage even more effective.

Young fawns have white spots on their back and sides.

A fawn crosses
a mossy stream.

Babies Sit Tight

In the early days of its life, a fawn needs much rest and a lot of milk. But to make the milk, the doe needs to eat. She can't eat and watch over her baby at the same time. So, she leaves the fawn in a safe place to rest while she feeds. She never goes too far away and comes back often to feed the fawn. If the doe has twins, she leaves each one in a different place. She does that because if a predator found them together, it will probably kill both of them. But if they are in different places and a predator finds one fawn, the other is likely to survive, undiscovered.

If you ever find a fawn lying in the grass alone, don't think its mother has abandoned it. She is most likely very close by, watching everything that happens. The best thing to do is to walk quietly away and leave the fawn alone.

Playtime for Fawns

After about three weeks of resting and feeding, the fawn is strong enough to go with its mother when she feeds. That is often its first chance to meet other fawns, and they can't wait to play! Their favorite game is "tag." They chase one another all over the place, leaping high in the air and sometimes even over one another! They try to chase other animals, too, such as rabbits or even crickets. Though they love to play, fawns know to obey their mother and always come quickly when she calls.

Words to Know

Antlers   The bony branches that grow on the head of male deer each year. Female caribou grow antlers, too.

Artiodactyla   A group of hoofed animals to which deer belong.

Browse   To feed on the leaves from trees and shrubs.

Bucks   Male deer.

Camouflage   Special patterns and colors that make an animal difficult to see against a particular background.

Does   Female deer.

Fawns   Baby deer.

Graze   To feed on grass.

Hoof	The hard, nail-like part of the foot of a bison, horse, sheep, or other hoofed animal.
Horns	Permanent headgear worn by some hoofed animals, but not by deer.
Mate	To come together to produce young.
Perissodactyla	A group of hoofed animals that includes horses, tapirs, and rhinos.
Predators	Animals that hunt other animals.
Preserve	An area of land in which certain wildlife is protected.
Velvet	The soft skin that covers new antlers until they finish growing.
Venison	The meat that comes from deer.
Yarding	When deer gather in groups in winter for safety.

Find Out More

Books

Biel, T. L. *Deer Family*. Zoobooks. Wildlife Education, Ltd: Poway, California, 1997.

Hinshaw, D. and W. Munoz. *White-tailed Deer*. Minneapolis, Minnesota: Lerner Publications, 2004.

Web sites

DesertUSA
www.desertusa.com/feb97/du_muledeer.html
Did you know that mule deer live in the deserts of the southwestern United States? Find out more here.

NatureWorks
www.nhptv.org/NatureWorks/whitetaileddeer.htm
Facts about white-tailed deer.

Index

52